The Perfect

X-CHANGE

Marcia Quainoo

ISBN 979-8-89043-158-5 (paperback)
ISBN 979-8-89043-159-2 (digital)

Christian Faith Publishing
832 Park Avenue
Meadville, PA 16335
www.christianfaithpublishing.com

Printed in the United States of America

March 7, 2023

Good morning, family. It is my prayer that this message finds you well. Hallelujah!

I am praising the Lord Almighty in advance for what only He has done, and I know by the spirit of the Lord, it is well. If you are wondering why I started this passage with a "good morning," please know that morning has come! Hallelujah! I believe. Let us believe together. It is my hope that you have invested in my first two testimonies. If not, it is never too late. This testimony will also bless you.

The moment has come for us, family, to shine brightly for the glory of God. The table is set. The moment has come for us to be perfected, as the body of Christ (bride of Christ Jesus, the church). The Lord has spoken from the beginning, "And God said, Let there be light: and there was light" (Genesis 1:3).

BEULAH HalleluYAH, the first installment of this trilogy, referenced the bride we are to become. A bride no longer forsaken or desolated. HalleluYAH! As the bride, when we die to self and submit to the will of God, we can become who God says we are. HalleluYAH!

The second book, *ONE Flesh*, referenced when the two became one for the glory of God Almighty. Actually, as I am writing this testimony, the second book is currently going through the final stages of production. The Lord is so amazing. Every script of these moments are contributed by the Spirit of the Lord. *Only God can do it, and He has done it*. I am just writing the script. It is all the Lord's Will for our lives to walk upright and obey His teachings. I know that the vessels, that this testimony is intended for, will be truly blessed. I know this because I believe the Word of the Lord. Amen.

This third book, *The Perfect X-CHANGE*, is hot off the press as well. I am totally submitted to the leading of the Holy Spirit this morning. I was actually intended to wait on the printing of the last book. However, when the Lord says yes, no one can say no. I have been given the go ahead to write this morning. So we are getting the opportunity to experience this walk together.

It is marvelous. It is refreshing to allow the Holy Spirit to move in such a way in our lives. One can totally get use to this benefit of being yielded to the Spirit of the Lord. It takes the burden off us and leaves the increase in harvest up to the Lord, *for His glory*. Will you believe with me for increase for obeying the voice of the Lord?

The Perfect X-CHANGE speaks for itself. It stands alone, *one* with the *father* and *son*, in the power of the Holy Spirit for the glory of God. It all makes perfect sense to me now. I was just telling my husband that this morning. The light, the greatest Light, has been turned on in my life. It is our prayer that you all are experiencing the same light, the greatest Light (Christ Jesus). HalleluYah! Singing, "His name is YAHWEH!" Family, I can only pray that you all are experiencing such glory this morning. Yes, it is morning time. It's a celebration of what we have been hoping for that has been poured out over this land, *BEULAH! HalleluYAH!* It is the Lord's doing. The Spirit of the Lord God is being poured out even now all across the land.

Get ready, family, for the celebration, *The Perfect X-CHANGE*. HalleluYAH! I will not share much with you from this point, only the instructions that the Lord has given me to share with you all. It is up to each one of us (the Lord Almighty children) to exercise our God-given rights in this earth and shine brightly. We always had all the help we needed to shine bright; however, it has been lying dormant in us far too long. The problem and the answer have always been within us. The answer has now prevailed. It was always tied to our willingness to receive, obey, declare, and believe the Word of Lord. Just as much as we have been seeking to fill that void in our lives; even more so, the Lord Almighty has been looking to fill that void. HalleluYAH!

The Holy Spirit just reminded me that the first testimony (*BEULAH HalleluYAH*), that we've witnessed together, was three years in making. The second testimony (*ONE Flesh*) was three months in making. This testimony (*The Perfect X-CHANGE*) is only one day, today, in the making.

Wow! Wow! Wow!

I am running in the spirit of the Lord because I am hearing this now, and you are also partakers of this experience. Yes, only God can perfect what's concerning his children. I believe the Lord is getting us ready for the LORD's day. The Word of God Almighty is now perfecting his children. His Word has told us that He will make a way in the wilderness for us. It is already done, even from the beginning.

Call to Remembrance

Remember,

Trust in the Lord with all thine heart; and, lean not unto thine own understanding. In all thy ways acknowledge him, and he shall direct thy paths. Be not wise in thine own eyes; fear the Lord, and depart from evil. (Proverbs 3:5–7)

Then said he, Lo, I come to do thy will, O God. He taketh away the first, that he may establish the second. By the which will we are sanctified through the offering of the body of Jesus Christ once for all. And every priest standeth daily ministering and offering oftentimes the same sacrifices, which can never take away sins. (Hebrews 10:9–11)

But this man, after he had offered one sacrifice for sins forever; sat down on the right had of God; From henceforth expecting till his enemies be made his footstool. For by one offering he hath perfected for ever them that are sanctified. (Hebrews 10:12–14)

Whereof the Holy Ghost also is a witness to us: for after that he had said before, This is the covenant that I will make with them after those days, saith the Lord, I will put my laws into their hearts, and in their minds will I write them; And their sins and iniquities will I remember no more. Now where remission of these is, there is no more offering for sin. (Hebrews 10:15–18)

Having therefore, brethren, boldness to enter into the holiest by the blood of Jesus, By a new and living way which he hath consecrated for us, through the veil, that is to say, his flesh; And having an high priest over the house of God; Let us draw near with a true heart in full assurance of faith, having our hearts sprinkled from an evil conscience, and our bodies washed with pure water. (Hebrews 10:19–22)

Let us hold fast the profession of our faith without wavering; (for he is faithful that promised;) And let us consider one another to provoke unto love and to good works: Not forsaking the assembling of ourselves together, as the manner of some is; but exhorting one another: and so much the more, as ye see the day approaching. (Hebrews 10:23–25)

Cast not away therefore your confidence, which hath great recompence of reward. For ye have need of patience, that, after ye have done the will of God, ye might receive the promise. For yet a little while, and he that shall come will come, and will not tarry. (Hebrews 10:35–37)

Now the just shall live by faith: but if any man draw back, my soul shall have no pleasure in him. But we are not of them who draw back unto perdition; but of them that believe to the saving of the soul. (Hebrews 10:38–39)

Now faith is the substance of things hoped for, the evidence of things not seen. For by it the elders obtained a good report. (Hebrews 11:1–2)

Let There Be Light

Testimony time. Just a couple of nights ago, I was finding it difficult to rest. Due to some cares on my heart for select people, I started to become physically unwell. My husband had notice the change and encourage me to relax, but I was finding it difficult. The cares were too much and came in like a flood. I thank the Lord that my husband was sensitive to what I was experiencing and stood with me in prayer. He prayed the prayer of faith with me, and I closed my eyes for rest. Somewhere in between me closing my eyes and opening my eyes the next morning, the answer came. I recall asking the Lord what is happening before closing my eyes; however, I couldn't remember the time that I slept. Upon waking up that morning, the spirit of the Lord reminded me of the scripture that talks about the light of the body is the eye. Hallelujah! This word encouraged me to seek this scripture out in the Bible along with other supporting scriptures. The Holy Spirit had interceded on my behalf and has reminded me, in retrospect, of the process of deliverance from the Word of God. The problem was the fact that I had allowed my mind to get overwhelmed by what I was seeing rather that what I know to be true, the Word.

Remember,

> The light of the body is the eye: if therefore
> thine eye be single, thy whole body shall be full
> of light. But if thine eye be evil, thy whole body
> shall be full of darkness. If therefore the light that

is in thee be darkness, how great is that darkness!
(Matthews 6:22–23).

> And God said, Let there be light: and there
> was light. And God saw the light, that it was
> good: and God divided the light from the dark-
> ness. And God called the light Day, and the dark-
> ness he called Night. And the evening and the
> morning were the first day. (Genesis 1:3–5)

> But the path of the just is as the shining
> light, that shineth more and more unto the per-
> fect day. (Proverbs 4:18)

> My son, attend to my words; incline thine
> ear unto my sayings. Let them not depart from
> thine eyes; keep them in the midst of thine heart.
> For they are life unto those that find them, and
> health to all their flesh. (Proverbs 4:20–22)

Once I realized the problem and applied the answer, as directed by the Word of God, the cares were lifted and burden made light. This reminded me of things that are not in my control, the importance of submitting everything unto the Lord in prayer, and keep my eyes full of the light so that my whole body can be full with light instead of darkness. The part that blessed me so is when it says in scripture, "And the evening and the morning were the first day" (Genesis 1:5b).

There are only three instructions that I am led to give you all on this journey, in hopes that it will bless you indeed as well. The pandemic of believing a lie over the truth ends *now*. It is more that I can say; however, I believe we all have to be more practical with our walk with Christ Jesus by evidence of searching out the answer to our problems daily. The Lord has already prepared the way for us. We just have to be sensitive to the voice of the Lord and obey His work even when the enemy tries to come in like a flood.

1. ASK
2. SEEK
3. KNOCK

Reference, Matthew 7:7
Remember,

> Behold, I send my Angel before thee, to keep thee in the way, and to bring thee into the place which I have prepared. Beware of him, and obey his voice, provoke him not; for he will not pardon your transgressions: for my name is in him. But if thou shalt indeed obey his voice, and do all that I speak; then I will be an enemy unto thine enemies, and an adversary unto thine adversaries. (Exodus 23:20–22)

For the remainder of this journey, I have included *The Perfect X-CHANGE* chart that will assist us in soul-tracking. The goal is to keep our eyes full of light and exercise our rights to the Word when tempted and tried. Remember, the spirit of the Lord and angel of the Lord is here to assist us. We are not alone; however, we must exercise our God given rights and obey God daily to experience *The Perfect X-CHANGE* from darkness to light.

X- DARKNESS (PROBLEM)

1. Worry

CHANGE- LIGHT (SCRIPTURE)

1. 1 Peter 5:7: "Cast all your worries (anxiety) on him because he cares for us."

X- DARKNESS (PROBLEM)

2. Depression

CHANGE- LIGHT (SCRIPTURE)

2. John 16:33: "I have told you these things, so that in me you may have peace. In this world, you will have trouble. But take heart! I have overcome the world."

X- DARKNESS (PROBLEM)

3. Paranoid Thoughts

CHANGE- LIGHT (SCRIPTURE)

3. 2 Timothy 1:7: "For God has not given us the spirit of fear; but of *power*, and of *love*, and of a *Sound mind*."

X- DARKNESS (PROBLEM)

CHANGE- LIGHT (SCRIPTURES)

X- DARKNESS (PROBLEM)

CHANGE- LIGHT (SCRIPTURES)

X- DARKNESS (PROBLEM)

CHANGE- LIGHT (SCRIPTURES)

NOTES:

THE PERFECT x-change CHART
(SOUL TRACKER)
DAY 2

X- DARKNESS (PROBLEM)

CHANGE- LIGHT (SCRIPTURES)

X- DARKNESS (PROBLEM)

CHANGE- LIGHT (SCRIPTURES)

X- DARKNESS (PROBLEM)

CHANGE- LIGHT (SCRIPTURES)

NOTES:

X- DARKNESS (PROBLEM)

CHANGE- LIGHT (SCRIPTURES)

X- DARKNESS (PROBLEM)

CHANGE- LIGHT (SCRIPTURES)

X- DARKNESS (PROBLEM)

CHANGE- LIGHT (SCRIPTURES)

NOTES:

X- DARKNESS (PROBLEM)

CHANGE- LIGHT (SCRIPTURES)

X- DARKNESS (PROBLEM)

CHANGE- LIGHT (SCRIPTURES)

X- DARKNESS (PROBLEM)

CHANGE- LIGHT (SCRIPTURES)

NOTES:

X- DARKNESS (PROBLEM)

CHANGE- LIGHT (SCRIPTURES)

X- DARKNESS (PROBLEM)

CHANGE- LIGHT (SCRIPTURES)

X- DARKNESS (PROBLEM)

CHANGE- LIGHT (SCRIPTURES)

NOTES:

X- DARKNESS (PROBLEM)

CHANGE- LIGHT (SCRIPTURES)

X- DARKNESS (PROBLEM)

CHANGE- LIGHT (SCRIPTURES)

X- DARKNESS (PROBLEM)

CHANGE- LIGHT (SCRIPTURES)

NOTES:

X- DARKNESS (PROBLEM)

CHANGE- LIGHT (SCRIPTURES)

X- DARKNESS (PROBLEM)

CHANGE- LIGHT (SCRIPTURES)

X- DARKNESS (PROBLEM)

CHANGE- LIGHT (SCRIPTURES)

NOTES:

THE PERFECT x-change CHART
(SOUL TRACKER)
DAY 8

X- DARKNESS (PROBLEM)

____

____

____

____

____

CHANGE- LIGHT (SCRIPTURES)

____

____

____

____

____

____

X- DARKNESS (PROBLEM)

____

____

____

____

____

CHANGE- LIGHT (SCRIPTURES)

____

____

____

____

____

X- DARKNESS (PROBLEM)

CHANGE- LIGHT (SCRIPTURES)

NOTES:

THE PERFECT x-change CHART
(SOUL TRACKER)
DAY 9

X- DARKNESS (PROBLEM)

CHANGE- LIGHT (SCRIPTURES)

X- DARKNESS (PROBLEM)

CHANGE- LIGHT (SCRIPTURES)

X- DARKNESS (PROBLEM)

CHANGE- LIGHT (SCRIPTURES)

NOTES:

X- DARKNESS (PROBLEM)

CHANGE- LIGHT (SCRIPTURES)

X- DARKNESS (PROBLEM)

CHANGE- LIGHT (SCRIPTURES)

X- DARKNESS (PROBLEM)

CHANGE- LIGHT (SCRIPTURES)

NOTES:

X- DARKNESS (PROBLEM)

X- DARKNESS (PROBLEM)

CHANGE- LIGHT (SCRIPTURES)

X- DARKNESS (PROBLEM)

CHANGE- LIGHT (SCRIPTURES)

X- DARKNESS (PROBLEM)

CHANGE- LIGHT (SCRIPTURES)

NOTES:

X- DARKNESS (PROBLEM)

CHANGE- LIGHT (SCRIPTURES)

X- DARKNESS (PROBLEM)

CHANGE- LIGHT (SCRIPTURES)

X- DARKNESS (PROBLEM)

CHANGE- LIGHT (SCRIPTURES)

NOTES:

THE PERFECT x-change CHART
(SOUL TRACKER)
DAY 13

X- DARKNESS (PROBLEM)

CHANGE- LIGHT (SCRIPTURES)

X- DARKNESS (PROBLEM)

CHANGE- LIGHT (SCRIPTURES)

X- DARKNESS (PROBLEM)

CHANGE- LIGHT (SCRIPTURES)

NOTES:

X- DARKNESS (PROBLEM)

CHANGE- LIGHT (SCRIPTURES)

X- DARKNESS (PROBLEM)

CHANGE- LIGHT (SCRIPTURES)

X- DARKNESS (PROBLEM)

CHANGE- LIGHT (SCRIPTURES)

NOTES:

THE PERFECT x-change CHART
(SOUL TRACKER)
DAY 15

X- DARKNESS (PROBLEM)

CHANGE- LIGHT (SCRIPTURES)

X- DARKNESS (PROBLEM)

CHANGE- LIGHT (SCRIPTURES)

X- DARKNESS (PROBLEM)

CHANGE- LIGHT (SCRIPTURES)

NOTES:

THE PERFECT x-change CHART
(SOUL TRACKER)
DAY 16

X- DARKNESS (PROBLEM)

CHANGE- LIGHT (SCRIPTURES)

X- DARKNESS (PROBLEM)

CHANGE- LIGHT (SCRIPTURES)

X- DARKNESS (PROBLEM)

CHANGE- LIGHT (SCRIPTURES)

NOTES:

X- DARKNESS (PROBLEM)

CHANGE- LIGHT (SCRIPTURES)

X- DARKNESS (PROBLEM)

CHANGE- LIGHT (SCRIPTURES)

X- DARKNESS (PROBLEM)

____

____

____

____

____

CHANGE- LIGHT (SCRIPTURES)

____

____

____

____

____

NOTES:

____

____

____

____

____

____

____

____

____

____

____

____

____

____

____

____

THE PERFECT x-change CHART
(SOUL TRACKER)
DAY 18

X- DARKNESS (PROBLEM)

CHANGE- LIGHT (SCRIPTURES)

X- DARKNESS (PROBLEM)

CHANGE- LIGHT (SCRIPTURES)

X- DARKNESS (PROBLEM)

CHANGE- LIGHT (SCRIPTURES)

NOTES:

X- DARKNESS (PROBLEM)

CHANGE- LIGHT (SCRIPTURES)

X- DARKNESS (PROBLEM)

CHANGE- LIGHT (SCRIPTURES)

X- DARKNESS (PROBLEM)

CHANGE- LIGHT (SCRIPTURES)

NOTES:

X- DARKNESS (PROBLEM)

CHANGE- LIGHT (SCRIPTURES)

X- DARKNESS (PROBLEM)

CHANGE- LIGHT (SCRIPTURES)

X- DARKNESS (PROBLEM)

CHANGE- LIGHT (SCRIPTURES)

NOTES:

X- DARKNESS (PROBLEM)

CHANGE- LIGHT (SCRIPTURES)

X- DARKNESS (PROBLEM)

CHANGE- LIGHT (SCRIPTURES)

X- DARKNESS (PROBLEM)

CHANGE- LIGHT (SCRIPTURES)

NOTES:

X- DARKNESS (PROBLEM)

CHANGE- LIGHT (SCRIPTURES)

X- DARKNESS (PROBLEM)

CHANGE- LIGHT (SCRIPTURES)

X- DARKNESS (PROBLEM)

CHANGE- LIGHT (SCRIPTURES)

NOTES:

X- DARKNESS (PROBLEM)

CHANGE- LIGHT (SCRIPTURES)

X- DARKNESS (PROBLEM)

CHANGE- LIGHT (SCRIPTURES)

X- DARKNESS (PROBLEM)

CHANGE- LIGHT (SCRIPTURES)

NOTES:

X- DARKNESS (PROBLEM)

CHANGE- LIGHT (SCRIPTURES)

X- DARKNESS (PROBLEM)

CHANGE- LIGHT (SCRIPTURES)

X- DARKNESS (PROBLEM)

CHANGE- LIGHT (SCRIPTURES)

NOTES:

X- DARKNESS (PROBLEM)

CHANGE- LIGHT (SCRIPTURES)

X- DARKNESS (PROBLEM)

CHANGE- LIGHT (SCRIPTURES)

X- DARKNESS (PROBLEM)

CHANGE- LIGHT (SCRIPTURES)

NOTES:

X- DARKNESS (PROBLEM)

CHANGE- LIGHT (SCRIPTURES)

X- DARKNESS (PROBLEM)

CHANGE- LIGHT (SCRIPTURES)

X- DARKNESS (PROBLEM)

CHANGE- LIGHT (SCRIPTURES)

NOTES:

X- DARKNESS (PROBLEM)

CHANGE- LIGHT (SCRIPTURES)

X- DARKNESS (PROBLEM)

CHANGE- LIGHT (SCRIPTURES)

X- DARKNESS (PROBLEM)

CHANGE- LIGHT (SCRIPTURES)

NOTES:

X- DARKNESS (PROBLEM)

CHANGE- LIGHT (SCRIPTURES)

X- DARKNESS (PROBLEM)

CHANGE- LIGHT (SCRIPTURES)

X- DARKNESS (PROBLEM)

CHANGE- LIGHT (SCRIPTURES)

NOTES:

X- DARKNESS (PROBLEM)

CHANGE- LIGHT (SCRIPTURES)

X- DARKNESS (PROBLEM)

CHANGE- LIGHT (SCRIPTURES)

X- DARKNESS (PROBLEM)

CHANGE- LIGHT (SCRIPTURES)

NOTES:

THE PERFECT x-change CHART
(SOUL TRACKER)
DAY 30

X- DARKNESS (PROBLEM)

____
____
____
____
____
____

CHANGE- LIGHT (SCRIPTURES)

____
____
____
____
____
____

X- DARKNESS (PROBLEM)

____
____
____
____
____
____

CHANGE- LIGHT (SCRIPTURES)

____
____
____
____
____
____

X- DARKNESS (PROBLEM)

CHANGE- LIGHT (SCRIPTURES)

NOTES:

THE PERFECT x-change CHART
(SOUL TRACKER)
DAY 31

X- DARKNESS (PROBLEM)

CHANGE- LIGHT (SCRIPTURES)

X- DARKNESS (PROBLEM)

CHANGE- LIGHT (SCRIPTURES)

X- DARKNESS (PROBLEM)

CHANGE- LIGHT (SCRIPTURES)

NOTES:

THE PERFECT x-change CHART
(SOUL TRACKER)
DAY 32

X- DARKNESS (PROBLEM)

CHANGE- LIGHT (SCRIPTURES)

X- DARKNESS (PROBLEM)

CHANGE- LIGHT (SCRIPTURES)

X- DARKNESS (PROBLEM)

CHANGE- LIGHT (SCRIPTURES)

NOTES:

X- DARKNESS (PROBLEM)

CHANGE- LIGHT (SCRIPTURES)

X- DARKNESS (PROBLEM)

CHANGE- LIGHT (SCRIPTURES)

X- DARKNESS (PROBLEM)

CHANGE- LIGHT (SCRIPTURES)

NOTES:

X- DARKNESS (PROBLEM)

CHANGE- LIGHT (SCRIPTURES)

X- DARKNESS (PROBLEM)

CHANGE- LIGHT (SCRIPTURES)

X- DARKNESS (PROBLEM)

CHANGE- LIGHT (SCRIPTURES)

NOTES:

X- DARKNESS (PROBLEM)

CHANGE- LIGHT (SCRIPTURES)

X- DARKNESS (PROBLEM)

CHANGE- LIGHT (SCRIPTURES)

X- DARKNESS (PROBLEM)

CHANGE- LIGHT (SCRIPTURES)

NOTES:

X- DARKNESS (PROBLEM)

CHANGE- LIGHT (SCRIPTURES)

X- DARKNESS (PROBLEM)

CHANGE- LIGHT (SCRIPTURES)

X- DARKNESS (PROBLEM)

CHANGE- LIGHT (SCRIPTURES)

NOTES:

X- DARKNESS (PROBLEM)

CHANGE- LIGHT (SCRIPTURES)

X- DARKNESS (PROBLEM)

CHANGE- LIGHT (SCRIPTURES)

X- DARKNESS (PROBLEM)

CHANGE- LIGHT (SCRIPTURES)

NOTES:

X- DARKNESS (PROBLEM)

CHANGE- LIGHT (SCRIPTURES)

X- DARKNESS (PROBLEM)

CHANGE- LIGHT (SCRIPTURES)

X- DARKNESS (PROBLEM)

CHANGE- LIGHT (SCRIPTURES)

NOTES:

X- DARKNESS (PROBLEM)

CHANGE- LIGHT (SCRIPTURES)

X- DARKNESS (PROBLEM)

CHANGE- LIGHT (SCRIPTURES)

X- DARKNESS (PROBLEM)

CHANGE- LIGHT (SCRIPTURES)

NOTES:

THE PERFECT x-change CHART
(SOUL TRACKER)
DAY 40

X- DARKNESS (PROBLEM)

CHANGE- LIGHT (SCRIPTURES)

X- DARKNESS (PROBLEM)

CHANGE- LIGHT (SCRIPTURES)

X- DARKNESS (PROBLEM)

CHANGE- LIGHT (SCRIPTURES)

NOTES:

X- DARKNESS (PROBLEM)

CHANGE- LIGHT (SCRIPTURES)

X- DARKNESS (PROBLEM)

CHANGE- LIGHT (SCRIPTURES)

X- DARKNESS (PROBLEM)

CHANGE- LIGHT (SCRIPTURES)

NOTES:

THE PERFECT x-change CHART (SOUL TRACKER) DAY 42

X- DARKNESS (PROBLEM)

CHANGE- LIGHT (SCRIPTURES)

X- DARKNESS (PROBLEM)

CHANGE- LIGHT (SCRIPTURES)

X- DARKNESS (PROBLEM)

CHANGE- LIGHT (SCRIPTURES)

NOTES:

THE PERFECT x-change CHART
(SOUL TRACKER)
DAY 43

X- DARKNESS (PROBLEM)

CHANGE- LIGHT (SCRIPTURES)

X- DARKNESS (PROBLEM)

CHANGE- LIGHT (SCRIPTURES)

X- DARKNESS (PROBLEM)

CHANGE- LIGHT (SCRIPTURES)

NOTES:

X- DARKNESS (PROBLEM)

CHANGE- LIGHT (SCRIPTURES)

X- DARKNESS (PROBLEM)

CHANGE- LIGHT (SCRIPTURES)

X- DARKNESS (PROBLEM)

CHANGE- LIGHT (SCRIPTURES)

NOTES:

X- DARKNESS (PROBLEM)

CHANGE- LIGHT (SCRIPTURES)

X- DARKNESS (PROBLEM)

CHANGE- LIGHT (SCRIPTURES)

X- DARKNESS (PROBLEM)

CHANGE- LIGHT (SCRIPTURES)

NOTES:

THE PERFECT x-change CHART
(SOUL TRACKER)
DAY 46

X- DARKNESS (PROBLEM)

CHANGE- LIGHT (SCRIPTURES)

X- DARKNESS (PROBLEM)

CHANGE- LIGHT (SCRIPTURES)

X- DARKNESS (PROBLEM)

CHANGE- LIGHT (SCRIPTURES)

NOTES:

X- DARKNESS (PROBLEM)

CHANGE- LIGHT (SCRIPTURES)

X- DARKNESS (PROBLEM)

CHANGE- LIGHT (SCRIPTURES)

X- DARKNESS (PROBLEM)

CHANGE- LIGHT (SCRIPTURES)

NOTES:

THE PERFECT x-change CHART
(SOUL TRACKER)
DAY 48

X- DARKNESS (PROBLEM)

____
____
____
____
____
____

CHANGE- LIGHT (SCRIPTURES)

____
____
____
____
____
____

X- DARKNESS (PROBLEM)

____
____
____
____
____
____

CHANGE- LIGHT (SCRIPTURES)

____
____
____
____
____
____

X- DARKNESS (PROBLEM)

CHANGE- LIGHT (SCRIPTURES)

NOTES:

X- DARKNESS (PROBLEM)

CHANGE- LIGHT (SCRIPTURES)

X- DARKNESS (PROBLEM)

CHANGE- LIGHT (SCRIPTURES)

X- DARKNESS (PROBLEM)

CHANGE- LIGHT (SCRIPTURES)

NOTES:

THE PERFECT x-change CHART
(SOUL TRACKER)
DAY 50

X- DARKNESS (PROBLEM)

CHANGE- LIGHT (SCRIPTURES)

X- DARKNESS (PROBLEM)

CHANGE- LIGHT (SCRIPTURES)

X- DARKNESS (PROBLEM)

CHANGE- LIGHT (SCRIPTURES)

NOTES:

X- DARKNESS (PROBLEM)

About the Author

Marcia Quainoo is a published author, wife, mother, minister, sister, and friend. As a nurse and mental health advocate, she has taken care of people throughout her twenty-five-year career. It is only befitting that Marcia has become a writer that pursues honoring God and helping his people. It is Marcia's desire that she creates paths and words that will inspire people to trust God and know Him personally. Marcia's previous work includes: *BEULAH HalleluYAH* and *ONE Flesh*.